75

Make Your
DREAM
Come True

CHARLES R.
SWINDO

...ET GUIDES™
Tyndale House Publishers, Inc.
Wheaton, Illinois

DD956182

Adapted from *Quest for Character*, copyright © 1987 by Charles R. Swindoll, Inc., Multnomah Press. Used by permission.

Scripture quotations, unless otherwise marked, are taken from the *New American Standard Bible*, © 1960, 1962, 1963, 1971, 1972, 1973, 1975, 1977 by The Lockman Foundation. Used by permission.

Pocket Guide is a trademark of Tyndale House Publishers, Inc.

Library of Congress Catalog Card Number 90-52194
ISBN 0-8423-7007-2
Copyright © 1990 by Charles R. Swindoll, Inc.
Printed in the United States of America

96 95 94 93 92 91 90
 9   8   7   6   5   4   3   2   1

CONTENTS

Profile of a Dreamer

Tom Fatjo is into garbage.

Oh, he hasn't always been. He used to be a quiet, efficient accounting executive. Another of those prim and proper Rice University grads who was going to play it straight, dodge all risk, and settle down easily into a life of the predictable. Boring but stable. Safe.

Everything was running along as planned until that night Tom found himself surrounded by a roomful of angry homeowners. As he sat among all those irritated people at the Willowbrook Civic Club in the southwestern section of Houston, his internal wheels began to turn.

You see, the city had refused to pick up their garbage at the back door of their homes. They had hired a private company to do it, but now that company was having serious problems. So the garbage was starting to stack up. And flies were everywhere, only adding to the sticky misery of that hot south Texas summer. Heated words flashed across the room.

And that night Tom Fatjo couldn't sleep.

A crazy idea kept rolling around in his head. A dream too unreal to admit to anyone but himself. A dream that spawned a series of incredible thoughts. That resulted in the purchase of a garbage truck. That led to a ten-year adventure you'd have trouble believing. That evolved into the largest solid-waste disposal company in the world, Browning-Ferris Industries, Inc. With annual sales in excess of (are you ready for this?) $500 *million*.

And that was only the beginning. Tom has also been instrumental in building over ten other companies—large companies—like the Criterion Capital Corporation, whose subsidiaries and affiliates manage well over $2 *billion*.

HOW DREAMS BEGIN
And to think it all started with a garbage truck.

No, a dream.

An unthinkable, scary, absolutely wild idea that refused to let him sleep. Getting up quietly so as not to awaken his wife, Diane, or his daughter, Tom sat down and stared out the window at the high, white moon. Just listen to his words:

At the time we were living on $750 a month. My partners and I had agreed when we started our accounting firm to conserve by living on reduced income, so I could certainly use some extra money. Increased income and solving the subdivision's garbage problems were my goals.

Next, I listed the financial information I would need to see if going into the garbage business would be feasible. I daydreamed some more about being a garbageman and laughed out loud as I pictured the look on people's faces when they heard that conservative Tom Fatjo with the white shirts and dark suits was driving a garbage truck. But excitement about doing this was much deeper than the allure of doing something different. I didn't know exactly why, but this crazy idea was suddenly very important to me.[1]

That's the way it is with dreams. Especially when God is in them. They appear crazy. (They *are* crazy!) Placed alongside the equiangular triangle of logic, cost, and timing, dreams are never congruent. They won't fly when you test them against the gravity of reality. And the strangest part of all: The more they are told "can't," the more they pulsate "can" and "will" and "must."

What's behind great accomplishments? Inevitably, great people. But what is in those "great people" that makes them different?

It's certainly not their age or sex or color or heritage or environment. No, it's got to be something inside their heads. They are people who *think* differently.

People whose ideas are woven into a meaningful pattern on the loom of dreams, threaded with colorful strands of imagination, creativity, even a touch of fantasy. They are among that band of young men the Scripture mentions "who will dream dreams and see visions."

THE DREAMER'S PARTNER

But there is another band of equally great people—they are the ones *married* to those modern-day seers! Whatever a dreamer gets into, so does his spouse. (Just be glad you're not a lady named Diane, who is expected to get into what her husband's into!)

My counsel to you is this: Give the dreamers room. Go easy on the "shouldn'ts" and the "can'ts," OK? Dreams are fragile things that have a hard time emerging in a cloud of negativism, reminders like "no money," and "too many problems." Have patience. Yours is a special calling. In fact, you're a partner in the process . . . so stay ready for anything. And I mean *anything!*

On May 24, 1965, a thirteen-and-a-half-foot boat slipped quietly out of the marina at Falmouth, Massachusetts. Its destination? England. It would be the smallest craft ever to make the voyage. Its name? *Tinkerbelle.* Its pilot? Robert Manry, a copyeditor for the *Cleveland Plain Dealer,* who felt that ten years at the desk was

Vision. It is essential for survival. It is spawned by faith, sustained by hope, sparked by imagination, and strengthened by enthusiasm. It is greater than sight, deeper than a dream, broader than an idea. Vision encompasses vast vistas outside the realm of the predictable, the safe, the expected. No wonder we perish without it! Ask God to stretch your vision today.

---

enough boredom for a while. So he took a leave of absence to fulfill his secret dream.

Manry was afraid . . . not of the ocean, but of all those people who would try to talk him out of the trip. So he didn't share it with many, just some relatives, and especially his wife, Virginia, his greatest source of support.

The trip? Anything but pleasant. He spent harrowing nights of sleeplessness trying to cross shipping lanes without getting run down and sunk. Weeks at sea caused his food to become tasteless. Loneliness, that age-old monster of the deep, led to terrifying hallucinations. His rudder broke three times. Storms swept him overboard, and had it not been for the rope he had knotted around his waist, he would never have been able to pull himself back on board. Finally, after seventy-eight days alone at sea, he sailed into Falmouth, England.

During those nights at the tiller, he had fantasized about what he would do once he arrived. He expected simply to check into a hotel, eat dinner alone, then the next morning see if perhaps the Associated Press might be interested in his story. Was he in for a surprise! Word of his approach had spread far and wide. To his amazement, three hundred vessels, with horns blasting, escorted *Tinkerbelle* into port. And forty thousand people stood screaming and cheering him to shore.

Robert Manry, the copyeditor turned dreamer, became an overnight hero. His story has been told around the world. But Robert couldn't have done it alone. Standing on the dock was an even greater hero—Virginia. Refusing to be rigid and closed back when Robert's dream was taking shape, she encouraged him on . . . willing to risk . . . allowing him the freedom to pursue his dream.

Go for It!

How many people stop because so few say, "Go!"

How few are those who see beyond the danger . . . who say to those on the edge of some venture, *"Go for it!"*

Funny, isn't it? I suppose it's related to one's inner ability to imagine, to envision, to be enraptured by the unseen, all hazards and hardships notwithstanding. I'm about convinced that one of the reasons mountain climbers connect themselves to one another with a rope is to keep the one on the end from going home. Guys out front never consider that as an option . . . but those in the rear—well, let's just say they are the last to get a glimpse of the glory. It's like a team of Huskies pulling a snowsled. The lead dog has a lot better view than the runt in the rear!

I've been thinking recently about how glad I am that certain visionaries refused to listen to the shortsighted doomsayers who could only see as far as the first obstacle. I'm glad, for example, that:

- Edison didn't give up on the light bulb even though his helpers seriously doubted the thing would ever work.

- Luther refused to back down when the Church doubled her fists and clenched her teeth.

- Michelangelo kept pounding and painting, regardless of those negative put-downs.

- Lindbergh decided to ignore what everyone else had said was ridiculous and flirted with death.

- Douglas MacArthur promised, during the darkest days of World War II, "I shall return."

- Papa ten Boom said yes to frightened Jews who needed a safe refuge, a hiding place in Holland.

- The distinguished Juilliard School of Music would see beyond the leg braces and wheelchair and admit an unlikely violin student named Perleman.

- Tom Sullivan decided to be everything that he could possibly be, even though he was born blind.

- The Gaithers made room in their busy lives for a scared young soprano named Sandi Patti who would one day thrill Christendom with songs like "We Shall Behold Him."

- Fred Dixon continued to train for the decathlon—and finished the course— even though critics told him he was over the hill.

- Jesus held nothing back when He left heaven, lived on earth, and went for it—all the way to the cross—and beyond.

You could add to the list. You may even belong on the list. If so, hats off to you.

VOTE YES!

But there's an unfinished part to this whole idea. Almost every day—certainly every week—we encounter someone who is in his or her own homemade boat, thinking seriously about sailing on the most daring, most frightening voyage of a lifetime. That person may be your marriage partner, or it may be a friend, someone you work with, a neighbor, perhaps a family member—your own child or brother, sister, parent. The ocean of possibilities is enormously inviting yet, let's face it, terribly threatening.

For most of us, the problem is not a lack of potential, it's a lack of perseverance . . . not a problem of having the goods but of hearing the bads. How very much could be accomplished if only there were more brave souls on the end of the pier urging us on, affirming us, regardless of the risks.

So when it comes to others, urge them on! Vote *yes!* Shout a rousing, "You are really something . . . I'm proud of you!" Dare to say what they need to hear the most: "Go for it!" Then pray like mad.

William Stafford, having been asked in an interview, "When did you decide to become a poet?" responded that the question was put wrongly: "Everyone is born a poet—a person discovering the way words sound and work, caring and delighting in words. I just kept on doing what everyone starts out doing. The real question is: Why did other people stop?"

My answer: They stopped because so few said, "Go!"

IN QUEST OF YOUR DREAM

What is *your* quest? Do you have a "lifelong dream"? Anything "dominating your life" enough to hold your attention for thirteen or more years? Some "adventurous journey" you'd love to participate in . . . some discovery you long to make . . . some enterprise you secretly imagine?

Without a quest, life is quickly reduced to bleak black and wimpy white, a diet too bland to get anybody out of bed in the morning. A quest fuels our fire. It refuses to let us drift downstream gathering debris. It keeps our mind in gear, makes us press on. All of us are surrounded by and benefit from the results of someone else's quest. Let me name a few:

- Above my head is a bright electric light. *Thanks, Edison.*

☞ Checkpoint

How easy it is to be "average." The ranks of the mediocre are crowded with status quo thinkers and predictable workers. How rare are those who live differently! Ask God to do a new work in you this day, to lift your sights above the expected, to develop in you the qualities that make for excellence. Then watch for those who may be struggling . . . perhaps dangerously near giving up. Give them a ready word of encouragement. Say, "Yes." Say, "Go!"

- On my nose are eyeglasses that enable me to focus. *Thanks, Franklin.*

- In my driveway is a car ready to take me wherever I choose to steer it. *Thanks, Ford.*

- Across my shelves are books full of interesting and carefully researched pages. *Thanks, authors.*

- Flashing through my mind are ideas, memories, stimulating thoughts, and creative skills. *Thanks, teachers.*

- Deep inside me are personality traits, strong convictions, a sense of right and wrong, a love for God, an ethical compass, a lifelong commitment to my wife and family. *Thanks, parents.*

- Tucked away in the folds of my life are discipline and determination, a refusal to quit when the going gets rough, a love for our country's freedom, a respect for authority. *Thanks, Marines.*

- Coming into my ears through the day are sounds of beautiful music, each piece representing a different mix of melody and rhythm . . . lyrics that linger. *Thanks, composers.*

- At home are peaceful and magnetic surroundings, eye-pleasing design, colorful wallpaper, tasteful and comfortable furnishings, hugs of affirmation, a shelter in a time of storm. *Thanks, Cynthia.*

My list could continue another page. So could yours. Because some cared enough to dream, to pursue, to follow through and complete their quest, our lives are more comfortable, more stable. If nothing else, that is enough to spur me on.

Building Dreams with Others

As we have seen, dreams aren't built alone. We need not only those who can encourage us but also those who share our vision. We can accomplish more together than we can by working apart.

John Stemmons, a well-known Dallas businessman, was asked to make a brief statement on what he considered to be foundational to developing a good team. His answer was crisp and clear. It is worth repeating.

> Find some people who are comers, who are going to be achievers in their own field . . . and people you can trust. Then grow old together.

Want a good illustration of that? The Billy Graham evangelistic team, the inner core of those gifted, great-hearted people whose names are now legendary among many. As I looked into the faces of this team in our church last Sunday, shook their hands, and felt warmed by their gracious smiles, it dawned on me that I cannot remember when they *weren't* together. It's almost as if they were born into the same family—or at least reared in the same neighborhood. In a day of job-hopping and a Lone Ranger mentality, it is refreshing to see such a group of capable and dedicated people, each one different and distinct, growing old together, yet still very much a solid team. They are all moving together toward the same dream.

Don't misread what it means to be a team. Group loyalty is not blind allegiance or harboring incompetence. Neither is it nepotistic prejudice that conveys the idea that everyone else is wrong except our little group. Nor is it so exclusive and so proud that it appears closed and secretive. Rather, there is freedom to be, to develop, to innovate, to make mistakes, to learn from one another . . . all the while feeling loved, supported, and affirmed.

Such a context has been called "management by friendship." Instead of suspicion and put-downs, there is trust that builds an *esprit de corps* within the team. Stress is held to a minimum since affection flows and laughter is encouraged. Who doesn't develop strong character—and the fruition of dreams—in a secure scene like that?

THE SECRET OF BUILDING TEAMS

In his best-seller, *American Caesar*, William Manchester introduces his readers to an in-depth acquaintance with Douglas MacArthur. He helps us feel closer to that strong personality as he digs beneath the intimidating exterior and unveils many of MacArthur's magnetic characteristics as well as strange quirks.

At one point, the author analyzes the remarkable loyalty that Colonel MacArthur elicited from his troops during World War I. By the time that war had ended, the man had won seven Silver Stars, two Distinguished Service Crosses, and also the coveted Distinguished Service Medal.

Obviously, those medals were partly due to his own bravery, but it cannot be denied that they were also due to another factor: his ability to educe a fierce loyalty from the men under his command. How did he pull that off? Here is Manchester's analysis in a nutshell:

- He was closer to their age than the other senior officers.

- He shared their discomforts and their danger.

- He adored them in return.[1]

Regardless of the man's well-publicized egomania and emotional distortions, Mac-

Arthur possessed a major redeeming virtue that eclipsed his flaws in his men's eyes and fired their passions: He genuinely and deeply cared for them. The word is *love*.

Nothing, absolutely nothing, pulls a team closer together or strengthens the lines of loyalty more than love. It breaks down internal competition. It silences gossip. It builds morale. It promotes feelings that say, "I belong" and "Who cares who gets the credit?" and "I must do my very best" and "You can trust me because I trust you."

Jesus' team of disciples was hardly the epitome of success when it got started. One would have wondered then why He selected such "a ragged aggregation of souls," as Robert Coleman tagged them.[2]

The genius of His plan was not immediately obvious. But by the end of the first century, no one would fault His selection. Except for Judas Iscariot, they were "comers," they proved themselves "achievers in their own field," and they became "people you can trust." Ultimately, they were responsible for turning their world upside down . . . or should I say right-side up? Whichever, no group in history has proven itself more effective than that first-century evangelistic team, the inner core of Christ's men.

Maybe you are in the process of putting together a group—a special team of people to accomplish some significant objectives or to advance your dream. Here are a couple of tips worth remembering. Instead of just going for big names or starting with a few hotshots, look for some comers, achievers in process, truly trustworthy folks. Love 'em to their full potential as you cultivate a long-haul friendship. Give your heart in unrestrained affection! Then watch what happens. A team drawn together by love and held together by grace has staying power.

Why It Takes Character

A long-time friend and mentor of mine died yesterday. He was a preacher *par excellence*. Trained in the old school. Always in a shirt and tie—with knot slim and tight. Three-piece suit, preferably. White shirt, well-pressed, heavy on the starch. Shoes shined. Every hair in place. Cleanly shaven. Trim. Immaculately tailored. And beneath all those externals? Character, solid as a stone.

His style of delivery? Strong. Dogmatic at times. Eloquent, often. Lots of alliteration with a memorized poem toward the end. Laced with illustrations that often began, "The story is told . . ." Never much humor, always dignified, a bit aloof, deep in thought, a voice in the lower register. Lots of leather-bound volumes in his library. Determined to hold high his call into ministry. Olive skin, deep eyes, straight teeth. Confident yet not arrogant. Handsome but not vain.

Never a hint of silly frivolity. Not the kind of man you'd expect to sit cross-legged in the front yard messing around with the kids. Or in the kitchen doing the dishes. Or changing the oil in his car. Or trying a back flip off the high dive. Or playing one-on-one in the driveway. The man had class.

It isn't that he was above all that, it's just that in his day, ministry-types maintained a sharp, straight edge. If he wasn't preaching, he was getting ready to. If he wasn't praying, he had just finished.

Frankly, I was never in his presence without feeling a sense of awe. Though a grown man, I sat up straight in his study and said "Sir" a lot. When he put his hand on my shoulder and prayed that God would "guide this young man" and "set him apart for the Master's use," I felt as if I had been knighted. He dripped with integrity. His counsel proved invincible. His thoughts and words were pristine pure—crisp and clean as a nun's habit. When he stepped behind a pulpit, he stood like a ramrod, polished and poised—surely one of the best in his day. He could have posed for the "Gentleman's Psalm," Psalm 15.

THINGS THAT CHANGE, THINGS THAT DON'T

But much of "his day" has passed. Today's approach with people is so very different. His was the era of Walter Winchell, George Patton, and Norman Rockwell. The no-monkey-business philosophy

☞ Checkpoint

God has a vision. Ever thought about that? The shape of His vision is set forth in the Bible where He promises to conform those who know Him to the image of Jesus.[1]

Saint Peter's second letter in the Bible goes so far as to *list* some of the things included in this image—diligence, faith, godliness, kindness, and love.[2]

In a word . . . character.

Character qualities in His children—that's God's vision. He won't quit His work until He completes His checklist. And when will that be? When we rest in peace . . . and not one day sooner. Only then will His mission be accomplished in us. We have Him to thank for not giving up on us as we go through the process of developing character. Thanks, God.

where lines were sharp, clearly defined, and speeches were one-way addresses. Dialogue was unheard of . . . the vulnerability of leaders? *Anathema*.

How times have changed! There isn't a profession that hasn't been forced to shift, making room for changes that are inevitable, many of them essential.

I thought of that recently while reading a job description given to floor nurses by a hospital in 1887. You who are nurses and physicians will smile at the list below in disbelief.

Anybody else glad there have been some changes since 1887?

Yes, times do change things . . . sometimes drastically. Styles change, as do expectations, salaries, communication systems, styles of relating to people, even preaching techniques.

But some things have no business changing. Like respect for authority, per-

---

NURSES' DUTIES IN 1887

In addition to caring for your fifty patients, each nurse will follow these regulations:

1. Daily sweep and mop the floors of your ward, dust the furniture and window sills.

2. Maintain an even temperature in your ward by bringing in a scuttle of coal for the day's business.

3. Light is important to observe the patient's condition. Therefore, each day fill kerosene lamps, clean chimneys, and trim wicks. Wash the windows once a week.

4. The nurse's notes are important in aiding the physician's work. Make your pens carefully; you may whittle nibs to your individual taste.

5. Each nurse on day duty will report every day at 7 A.M. and leave at 8 P.M., except on the Sabbath, on which day you will be off from 12 noon to 2 P.M.

6. Graduate nurses in good standing with the director of nurses will be given an

sonal integrity, wholesome thoughts, pure words, clean living, distinct roles of masculinity and femininity, commitment to Christ, love for family, and authentic servanthood. Character qualities are never up for grabs. That's why we're going to look at critical character qualities in the next few chapters. They are essential for those of us who want to make our dreams come true.

My friend and mentor is gone. Much of his style has left with him. But the deep-

---

evening off each week for courting purposes or two evenings a week if you go regularly to church.

7. Each nurse should lay aside from each payday a goodly sum of her earnings for her benefits during her declining years so that she will not become a burden. For example, if you earn $30 a month, you should set aside $15.

8. Any nurse who smokes, uses liquor in any form, gets her hair done at a beauty shop, or frequents dance halls will give the director of nurses good reason to suspect her worth, intentions, and integrity.

9. The nurse who performs her labors and serves her patients and doctors faithfully and without fault for a period of five years will be given an increase by the hospital administration of five cents a day, providing there are no hospital debts that are outstanding.

down stuff that made him great—ah, may that never be forgotten. Times must change. But character? Not on your life . . . or death.

Dream Builder: Gumption

We don't hear much about gumption any more. Too bad, since we need it more than ever these days. I was raised on gumption (sometimes called "spizzerinctum") and to this day I will use the word around the house . . . especially when trying to motivate the kids. I ran across it again while reading Robert Pirsig's *Zen and the Art of Motorcycle Maintenance* (now there's a great book title) as he was singing the praises of all that gumption represents. He writes:

> I like the word "gumption" because it's so homely and so forlorn and so out of style it looks as if it needs a friend and isn't likely to reject anyone who comes along. It's an old Scottish word, once used a lot by pioneers, but . . . seems to have all but dropped out of use. . . .
>
> A person filled with gumption doesn't sit around dissipating and stewing about things. He's at the front of the train of his

own awareness, watching to see what's up the track and meeting it when it comes.[1]

A little later Pirsig applies it to life, hiding his comments behind the word picture of repairing a motorcycle:

> If you're going to repair a motorcycle, an adequate supply of gumption is the first and most important tool. If you haven't got that you might as well gather up all the other tools and put them away, because they won't do you any good.
>
> Gumption is the psychic gasoline that keeps the whole thing going. If you haven't got it, there's no way the motorcycle can possibly be fixed. But if you have got it and know how to keep it, there's absolutely no way in the whole world that motorcycle can keep from getting fixed. It's bound to happen. Therefore the thing that must be monitored at all times and preserved before anything else is gumption.[2]

Seems a shame the old word has dropped through the cracks, especially since quitting is now more popular than finishing. I agree with that author, who'd like to start a whole new academic field on the subject. Can't you just see this entry in some college catalog: "Gumptionology 101." That'll never be, however, since gumption is better caught than taught. As is true of most other character traits, it is woven so subtly into the fabric of one's life that few ever stop and identify it. It is hidden like thick steel bars in concrete columns supporting ten-lane freeways. Gumption may be hidden, but it's an important tool for getting a job done.

HOW GUMPTION WORKS

Gumption enables us to save money rather than spend every dime we make. It keeps us at a hard task, like building a tedious model or completing an add-on or practicing piano or losing weight—and keeping it lost. Most folks get a little gumption in their initial birth packet, but it's a tool that rusts rather quickly. Here's some sandpaper:

1. *Gumption begins with a firm commitment.* Instead of starting with a bang, it's the human tendency to ponder, to rethink, to fiddle around with an idea until it's

awash in a slimy swamp of indefiniteness. An old recipe for a rabbit dish starts out, "First, catch the rabbit." That puts first things first. No rabbit, no dish. You want gumption to continue to the end? Start strong! We could well follow the example of the Bible prophet Isaiah who said he "set his face like flint," which is another way of saying he firmly decided.[4]

2. *Gumption means being disciplined one day at a time.* Rather than focusing on the whole enchilada, take it in bite-size chunks. The whole of any objective can overwhelm even the most courageous. Writing a book? Do so one page at a time. Running a marathon? Those 26-plus miles are run one step at a time. Trying to master a new language? Try one word at a time. There are 365 days in the average year. Divide any project by 365 and it doesn't seem all that intimidating, does it? It will take daily discipline, not annual discipline.

3. *Gumption includes being alert to subtle temptations.* Robert Pirsig referred to our being at the front of the train of our own awareness, looking up the track, and being ready to meet whatever comes. The Proverbs in the Bible contain some good advice: Gumption plans ahead . . . watching out for associations that weaken us, procrastination that steals from us, and rationalizations that lie to us.[5]

People who achieve their goals stay

alert. If it were possible for God to die and He died this morning, some wouldn't know it for three or four days. Gumption stabs us awake, keeps us wide-eyed and ready.

4. *Gumption requires the encouragement of accountability.* People—especially close friends—keep our tanks pumped full of enthusiasm. They communicate "You can do it, you can make it" a dozen different ways. People need people, which is why King Solomon came on so strong in stating that as iron sharpens iron, so people sharpen each other.[6]

5. *Gumption comes easier when we remember that finishing has its own unique rewards.* Those who only start projects never know the surge of satisfaction that comes with slapping hands together, wiping away those beads of perspiration, and saying that beautiful four-letter word, "Done!" Desire accomplished is sweet to the soul.

Dream Builder: Determination

Stingrays have always frightened me. Not the kind you drive but the kind that swim. Having been raised near the salt water and having fished all my life, I've had numerous encounters with creatures of the sea. Most of them are fascinating to watch, fun to catch, and delicious to eat.

But stingrays? No, thanks. I don't care if Jacques Cousteau's men *do* ride on their backs. I am comfortable in only one place if those ugly, flat beasts are in the water— and that's out of the water. Perhaps that explains why the following story from a recent article in the *Los Angeles Times* immediately caught my eye.

OCEANSIDE—It was a warm summer day in 1973, and Brian Styer was wading in shallow Pacific waters, bound for another session of surfing north of Scripps Pier in La Jolla.

Suddenly, he saw a shadow moving toward him beneath the waves. It was a stingray—with a wingspan later estimated at seventeen feet. And with a lightning-quick flip of the tail, the venomous sea creature fired its sharp barb through the surfer's left kneecap and out the back of his leg.

For ten days, Styer, then eighteen, lay partially paralyzed, wondering if he would ever walk again. He did, after doctors removed a portion of the barb, declared him fit, and released him from the hospital.

But a sliver of the stingray's weaponry escaped detection by X rays and remained lodged in Styer's knee for more than a year, causing a fierce infection that gradually invaded the surfer's entire leg, eroding muscle and bone surrounding the knee joint. He nearly lost the limb.

Twelve years and fourteen operations later, Styer is back on his board—dancing across the tops of waves with the help of a custom-made alloy brace that supports and strengthens his virtually useless knee.

And this week, after countless hours of practice, Styer realized his lifelong dream and qualified for a professional surfing contest—the world-famous Stubbies Pro International Surfing Tournament in Oceanside. His goal: To catch the eye of a sponsor and become the first disabled competitor on the pro surfing circuit.

Joining the pro tour will be no small accomplishment. For one thing, the condition of Styer's knee and the pain it causes him restrict his maneuvers and limit the length of time he can remain in the water. In addition, surfing sponsors are few, and those few may be reluctant to bet their bucks on a competitor who is 29—considered over the hill in the grueling water sport—and whose physical condition isn't 100 percent.

There is another problem. The massive doses of drugs used years ago to battle the infection creeping through Styer's body so weakened his immunity that the surfer has a 60 percent chance of contracting bacterial cancer in the leg. He is also highly susceptible to new infections, which flare up and require hospital care once every two months. A serious infection could resist treatment and force doctors to amputate.

The damage inflicted by the festering wound caused another obstacle to Styer's dreams of surfing prowess—pain. For almost ten years, the surfer relied on heavy doses of Percodan, Demerol, and other potent drugs to help him live with the pain, which is constant and is aggravated by walking, climbing stairs, and other movements.

Finally, feeling "like a vegetable" and convinced the narcotics "would kill me," Styer attended a workshop on living with pain and successfully weaned himself from the drugs. He now conducts similar pain courses at area hospitals.

These days, he relies on a wide array of measures to minimize the pain, including icing the knee, biofeedback, ultrasound, and physical therapy. And while he sleeps each night, he wears a neurostimulator that essentially blocks the electrical impulses that inform the brain of the pain in his knee.[1]

TWO QUESTIONS FOR DREAMERS

Drawing upon Styer's story, let me ask you a couple of personal questions.

First, what is your "lifelong dream"? Down deep inside your head, what hidden goal do you long to achieve? Think. State it to yourself. Picture it in your mind.

Second, how is your determination? Be honest. Have you started slacking off? Allowed a few obstacles to weaken your determination?

The surfer story speaks for itself, especially to me. If that guy will go through all that to accomplish his dream.... what can I say? Bring on the stingrays, Lord!

Uh, on second thought, Lord, could You maybe strengthen me by using only *freshwater* obstacles?

Dream Builder: Generosity

In our pocket of society where pampered affluence is rampant, we are often at a loss to know what kind of gifts to buy our friends and loved ones on special occasions. For some people (especially those who "have everything"), the standard type gift won't cut it. Nothing in the shopping mall catches our fancy.

I have a suggestion. It may not seem that expensive or sound very novel, but believe me, it works every time. It's one of those gifts that has great value but no price tag. It can't be lost and it never will be forgotten. No problem with size either. It fits all shapes, any age, and every personality. This ideal gift is . . . *yourself.* In your quest for your dream, don't forget the value of unselfishness.

That's right, give some of yourself away.

Give an hour of your time to someone who needs you. Give a note of encouragement to someone who is down. Give a hug of affirmation to someone in your family. Give a visit of mercy to someone who is laid aside. Give a meal you prepared to someone who is sick. Give a word of compassion to someone who just lost a mate. Give a deed of kindness to someone who is slow and easily overlooked. Jesus, the greatest giver who lived, taught: " . . . to the extent that you did it to one of these brothers of Mine, even the least of them, you did it to Me."[1]

TEDDY'S STORY

Teddy Stallard certainly qualified as "one of the least." Disinterested in school. Musty, wrinkled clothes. Hair never combed. One of those kids in school with a deadpan face, expressionless—sort of a glassy, unfocused stare. When Miss Thompson spoke to Teddy, he always answered in monosyllables. Unattractive, unmotivated, and distant, he was just plain hard to like. Even though his teacher said she loved all in her class the same, down inside she wasn't being completely truthful.

Whenever she marked Teddy's papers, she got a certain perverse pleasure out of putting Xs next to the wrong answers, and when she put the Fs at the top of the papers, she always did it with a flair. She should have known better; she had Teddy's records and she knew more about him than she wanted to admit. The records read:

1st Grade: Teddy shows promise with his work and attitude, but poor home situation.

2nd Grade: Teddy could do better. Mother is seriously ill. He receives little help at home.

3rd Grade: Teddy is a good boy but too serious. He is a slow learner. His mother died this year.

4th Grade: Teddy is very slow, but well-behaved. His father shows no interest.

Christmas came and the boys and girls in Miss Thompson's class brought her Christmas presents. They piled their presents on her desk and crowded around to watch her open them. Among the presents there was one from Teddy Stallard. She was surprised that he had brought her a gift, but he had. Teddy's gift was wrapped in brown paper and was held together with Scotch tape. On the paper were written the simple words, "For Miss Thompson from Teddy." When she opened Teddy's present, out fell a gaudy rhinestone bracelet, with half the stones missing, and a bottle of cheap perfume.

The other boys and girls began to giggle and smirk over Teddy's gifts, but Miss Thompson at least had enough sense to silence them by immediately putting on the bracelet and putting some of the perfume on her wrist. Holding her wrist up for the other children to smell, she said, "Doesn't it smell lovely?" And the children, taking their cue from the teacher, readily agreed with "oo's" and "ah's."

At the end of the day, when school was over and the other children had left, Teddy lingered behind. He slowly came over to her desk and said softly, "Miss Thompson . . . Miss Thompson, you smell just like my mother . . . and her bracelet looks real pretty on you, too. I'm glad you liked my presents." When Teddy left, Miss Thompson got down on her knees and asked God to forgive her.

The next day when the children came to school, they were welcomed by a new teacher. Miss Thompson had become a different person. She was no longer just a teacher; she had become an agent of God. She was now a person committed to loving her children and doing things for them that would live on after her. She helped all the children, but especially the slow ones, and especially Teddy Stallard. By the end of that school year, Teddy showed dramatic improvement. He had caught up with most of the students and was even ahead of some.

She didn't hear from Teddy for a long time. Then one day she received a note that read:

Dear Miss Thompson:
I wanted you to be the first to know.
I will be graduating second in my class.
Love,
Teddy Stallard

Four years later, another note came:

Dear Miss Thompson:
They just told me I will be graduating first in my class. I wanted you to be the first to know. The university has not been easy, but I liked it.
Love,
Teddy Stallard

And four years later:

Dear Miss Thompson:
As of today, I am Theodore Stallard, M.D. How about that? I wanted you to be the first to know. I am getting married next month, the 27th to be exact. I want you to come and sit where my mother would sit if she were alive. You are the only family I have now; Dad died last year.
Love,
Teddy Stallard

Miss Thompson went to that wedding and sat where Teddy's mother would have sat. She deserved to sit there; she had done something for Teddy that he could never forget.[2]

What can *you* give as a gift? Instead of giving only something you buy, risk giving something that will live on after you. Be really generous. Give yourself to a Teddy Stallard, "one of the least," whom you can help to become one of the greats.

Dream Builder: Honesty

- **Shoplifters will be prosecuted to the full extent of the law.**
- **Shoplifting is stealing. Stop it!**
- **All merchandise in this store is more expensive now than ever because of shoplifting. Help us fight inflation. Stop shoplifting.**
- **Shoplifters . . . Don't!**

I counted a dozen such signs in the same store yesterday. The shelves had been completely rearranged and the front door bolted shut permanently, forcing all customers to enter and exit inconveniently through a narrow aisle near the rear door by the cash register.

Why? Dishonesty. The manager confessed:

We were getting ripped off, frankly. Children, mothers, businessmen, blue-collar workers . . . professionals . . . you name it! Some shelves were stripped bare by closing time.

Last week I read about a woman, apparently pregnant, who walked out of the grocery store. Suspicious, the assistant manager stopped her. She later "gave birth" to a pound of butter, a chuck roast, a bottle of pancake syrup, two tubes of toothpaste, hair tonic, and several bars of candy. One California homemaker was observed tapping various articles as she made her way through a supermarket, followed by her two children who quickly pocketed the designated items.

Sophisticated alarm systems, one-way mirrors, locking devices, moving cameras, and electronic tape signals work hard at monitoring and exposing the problem . . . but it only grows larger. One estimate says that one out of every fifty-two customers every day carries away at least one unpaid-for item. The loss as of this writing is now an astronomical $3 billion annually . . . and rising.

THE COST OF DISHONESTY.
Now let's remember that shoplifting is merely one thin slice of humanity's stale cake of dishonesty. Don't forget our depraved track record: cheating on exams, taking a towel from the hotel, not working a full eight hours, bald-faced lies and half

truths, exaggerated statements, hedging on reports of losses covered by insurance companies, broken financial promises, domestic deceit, and (dare I mention) ye olde IRS reports we *sign* as being the truth. Did you know that ever since 1811 (when someone who had defrauded the government anonymously sent $5 to Washington, D.C.) the U.S. Treasury has operated a *Conscience Fund?* Since that time almost $3.5 million has been received from guilt-ridden citizens.

No dream is worth the cost of dishonesty. Any illegal or less-than-honest shortcut to success will carry a high price tag—for you or for someone else. The only answer to that cost, simplistic though it may seem, is a return to honesty. Integrity may be an even better word.

It would be a tough reversal for some, but oh, how needed! It boils down to an internal decision. Nothing less will counteract dishonesty. External punishment may hurt, but it doesn't solve.

It's my understanding that in some Arab communities when they catch a man stealing, they cut off his hand. You might think that would be sufficient to curb national dishonesty. But from what we read, it could hardly be said the Arabs have any corner on integrity.

Cutting off a hand to stop stealing misses the heart of the problem by about twenty-four inches. Dishonesty doesn't start in the hand any more than greed starts in the eye. It's an internal disease. It reveals a serious character flaw.

CULTIVATING HONESTY

Ideally, we plant the seeds and cultivate the roots of honesty in the *home*. Under the watchful eyes of consistent, diligent, persistent parents! In the best laboratory of life God ever designed—the family unit. It is *there* a proper scale of values is imbibed as the worth of a dollar is learned. It is on that anvil that the appreciation for hard work, the esteem for truth, the reward for achievement, and the cost of dishonesty are hammered out so that a life is shaped correctly down deep inside. Down where character is forged.

But what if you weren't so trained? Is there any hope?

Certainly! One of the reasons Christianity is so appealing is the hope it provides. Christ doesn't offer a technique on rebuilding *your* life. He offers you *His* life—His honesty, His integrity. Not a lot of rules and don'ts and threats. But sufficient power to counteract your dishonest bent. He calls it "a new nature, created after the likeness of God."[1]

Thoroughly honest.

Some would tell you that believing in Jesus Christ—trusting Him to break old habits and make you honest—means cutting off your head. Committing intellectual suicide. Is operating your inner life on the faith principle (instead of failure) wishful thinking? No way! It is not only the best way to stop being dishonest, it's the *only* way.

You need cut off neither your hand nor your head to become an honest person. What you want to cut off is your *habit of dishonesty* by allowing Christ to be the honored Presence throughout your inner home.

It won't be long before you find that honesty is the Guest policy.

CHAPTER 9

Dream Breaker:
Fear

It happened over forty years ago. The irony of it, however, amazes me to this day.

A mural artist named J. H. Zorthian read about a tiny boy who had been killed in traffic. His stomach churned as he thought of that ever happening to one of his three children. His worry became an inescapable anxiety. The more he imagined such a tragedy, the more fearful he became. His effectiveness as an artist was put on hold once he started running scared.

At last he surrendered to his obsession. Canceling his negotiations to purchase a large house in busy Pasadena, California, he began to seek a place where his children would be safe. His pursuit became so intense that he set aside all his work while scheming and planning every possible means to protect his children from harm.

He tried to imagine the presence of danger in everything. The location of the residence was critical. It must be sizable and remote, so he bought twelve acres perched on a mountain at the end of a long, winding, narrow road. At each turn along the road he posted signs: Children at Play. Before starting construction on the house itself, Zorthian personally built and fenced a play yard for his three children. He built it in such a way that it was impossible for a car to get within fifty feet of it.

Next . . . the house. With meticulous care he blended beauty and safety into the place. He put into it various shades of the designs he had concentrated in the murals he had hanging in forty-two public buildings in eastern cities. Only this time his objective was more than colorful art . . . most of all, it had to be safe and secure. He made sure of that. Finally, the garage was to be built. Only one automobile ever drove into that garage—Zorthian's.

He stood back and surveyed every possibility of danger to his children. He could think of only one remaining hazard. He had to back out of the garage. He might, in some hurried moment, back over one of the children. He immediately made plans for a protected turnaround. The contractor returned and set the forms for that additional area, but before the cement could be poured a downpour stopped the project. It was the first rainfall in many weeks of a long West Coast drought.

If it had not rained that week, the concrete turnaround would have been completed and been in use by Sunday. That was February 9, 1947 . . . the day his eighteen-month old son, Tiran, squirmed away from his sister's grasp and ran behind the car as Zorthian drove it from the garage. *The child was killed instantly.*

THE SHORTEST ROUTE TO INEFFECTIVENESS

There are no absolute guarantees. No failsafe plans. No perfectly reliable designs. No completely risk-free arrangements. Life refuses to be that neat and clean. Not even the neurotics, who go to extreme measures to make positively sure, are protected from their obsessive fears. Those "best laid plans of mice and men" continue to backfire, reminding us that living and risking go hand in hand. Running scared invariably blows up in one's face. All who fly risk crashing. All who drive risk colliding. All who run risk falling. All who walk risk stumbling. All who live risk *something*.

To laugh is to risk appearing the fool.
To weep is to risk appearing sentimental.

To reach out for another is to risk involvement.

To expose feelings is to risk exposing your true self.

To love is to risk not being loved in return.

To hope is to risk despair.

To try is to risk failure.

Want to know the shortest route to ineffectiveness? Start running scared. Try to cover every base at all times. Become paranoid over your front, your flanks, and your rear. Think about every possible peril, focus on the dangers, concern yourself with the "what ifs" instead of the "why nots." Take no chances. Say no to courage and yes to caution. Expect the worst. Play your cards close to your vest. Let fear run wild. "To him who is in fear," said Sophocles, "everything rustles." Triple lock all doors. Keep yourself safely tucked away in the secure nest of inaction. And before you know it (to borrow from the late author, E. Stanley Jones), "the paralysis of analysis" will set in. So will loneliness, and finally isolation. No thanks!

How much better to take on a few ornery bears and lions, like the ancient Israeli king David did. They ready us for giants like Goliath. How much more interesting to set sail for Jerusalem, like the famous apostle Paul, "not knowing what will happen to me there,"[1] than to spend one's days in a monotonous seaport, listening for footsteps and watching dull sunsets.

Guard yourself from overprotection!

Happily, not all have opted for safety. Some have overcome, regardless of the risks. Some have merged into greatness despite adversity. They refuse to listen to their fears. Nothing anyone says or does holds them back. Disabilities and disappointments need not disqualify! As Ted Engstrom insightfully writes:

> Cripple him, and you have a Sir Walter Scott. Lock him in a prison cell, and you have a John Bunyan. Bury him in the snows of Valley Forge, and you have a George Washington. Raise him in abject poverty, and you have an Abraham Lincoln. Strike him down with infantile paralysis, and he becomes Franklin Roosevelt. Burn him so severely that the doctors say he'll never walk again, and you have a Glenn Cunningham—who set the world's one-mile record in 1934. Deafen him, and you have a Ludwig van Beethoven. Have him or her born black in a society filled with racial discrimination, and you have a Booker T. Washington, a Marian Anderson, a George Washington Carver. . . . Call him a slow learner, "retarded," and write him off as uneducable, and you have an Albert Einstein.[2]

Tell your fears where to get off; otherwise, your dreams will be tarnished. Effectiveness—sometimes greatness—awaits those who refuse to run scared.

Dream Breaker: Unchecked Curiosity

"Curious George" is a monkey. He's the main character in a series of children's books that my oldest son used to love as a lad. We sat by the hour during his childhood and laughed like crazy at the outlandish predicaments little George experienced simply because his curiosity got the best of him.

The stories always followed the same basic pattern. George would casually drift into a new area, his inquisitive nature prompting him to investigate. The first step was neither wrong nor harmful, just a bit questionable. Invariably, George would not be satisfied with his initial encounter and discoveries, but would probe deeper . . . peer longer . . . pry further . . . until the novelty of the situation took on a new dimension—the dimension of *danger*.

Ultimately, nothing short of tragedy occurred—and the one who suffered the most was our dear little long-tailed friend, a curious primate named George.

THE BENEFITS OF CURIOSITY

Curiosity—at one point the sign of a healthy, sometimes ingenious mind . . . the spark that drives hungry seekers into the labyrinth of truth, refusing to stop short of thorough examination.

Curiosity—that time-worn gate hinged by determination and discipline that leads to the ecstasy of discovery through the agony of pursuit.

Curiosity—the built-in teacher that instantly challenges the status quo . . . that turns a wayward waif into a Churchill, a hopeless mute into a Keller, and a Missouri farm boy into a Disney.

Curiosity—the quality most often squelched in children by thoughtless, hurried adults who view questions as "interruptions" rather than the driving desire to lift one's mental wheels beyond the weary rut of the known.

WHEN CURIOSITY DOES MORE HARM THAN GOOD

But what a deceitful role it can play!

Remove the safety belt of moral and ethical parameters and curiosity will send our vehicle of learning on a collision course, destined for disaster. It has a way of making us meddle in others' affairs, for

curiosity is by nature intrusive.
wrong in the most attractive
known to man. It hides the damna.
sequences of adultery behind the a.
attire of excitement, soft music, an
warm embrace. It masquerades the hea
aches of drug abuse and alcoholism b
dressing them in the Levis and sweater of
a handsome, adventurous sailboat skipper.

Curiosity is the single, most needed
commodity depended upon to keep the
world of the occult busy and effective. It
alone is sufficient reason for the box-office
triumphs of movies that major on sadistic
violence or demonic encounters. Remove
curiosity from the heart and *The Exorcist* is
a sick joke . . . and even the Church of
Satan is laughed to scorn.

But it *cannot be removed!* Curiosity is as
much a part of your human nature as your
elbow is a part of your arm. It started with
Eve . . . and it continues with you. If your
curiosity sits up and leans forward, it's
only a matter of time before it wants to
move in—sometimes to your detrimer
And then there's no relying on the clai
"The devil made me do it!"

Saint James saw it clearly and said
straight:

Let no one say when he is tempted, "I
being tempted by God"; for God cannot
tempted by evil, and He Himself does
tempt anyone. But each one is temp
when he is carried away and enticed by

own lust. Then when lust has conceived, it gives birth to sin; and when sin is accomplished, it brings forth death.[1]

Fortunately, we need not be the victims of our foolish curiosity. Powerful help is available to guide us through the maze of mirages, booby traps, and landmines that would cause us to misuse our curiosity to our own harm and the demolition of our dreams. Jesus Christ, God in human form, has already walked the course we're walking now—and knows how to guide us through it unscathed.

By walking at His side, you can get the monkey off your back . . . even if its name isn't George.

The Power of Two Minutes

Depth, not length, is important. Not how long you take to talk but how much you say. Not how flowery and eloquent you sound but how sincerely and succinctly you speak . . . that's what is important . . . that's what is remembered. Two memorable minutes can be more effective than two marathon hours.

Step into the time tunnel and travel back with me to a field in Pennsylvania. The year is 1863. The month is July. The place is Gettysburg. Today it is a series of quiet rolling hills full of markings and memories. But back then it was a battleground . . . more horrible than we can imagine.

During the first days of that month, 51,000 were killed, wounded, or missing in what would prove the decisive Union victory of the Civil War. Anguished cries of the maimed and dying made a wailing chorus as the patients were hurried to improvised operating tables. One nurse recorded these words in her journal: "For seven days the tables literally ran with blood." Wagons and carts were filled to overflowing with amputated arms and legs, wheeled off to a deep trench, dumped, and buried. Preachers quoted the Twenty-third Psalm over and over as fast as their lips could say it while brave soldiers breathed their last.

The aftermath of any battlefield is always grim, but this was one of the worst. A national cemetery was proposed. A consecration service was planned. The date was set: November 19. The commission invited none other than the silver-tongued Edward Everett to deliver the dedication speech. Known for his cultured words, patriotic fervor, and public appeal, the orator, a former congressman and governor of Massachusetts, was a natural for the historic occasion. Predictably, he accepted.

In October President Lincoln announced his intentions to attend the ceremonies. This startled the commissioners, who had not expected Mr. Lincoln to leave the Capitol in wartime. Now, how could he not be asked to speak? They were nervous, realizing how much better an orator Everett was than Lincoln. Out of courtesy, they wrote the President on November 2, asking him to deliver "a few appropriate remarks."

AN "ILL-PREPARED SPEECH"

Certainly Lincoln knew the invitation was an afterthought, but it mattered little. When the battle of Gettysburg had begun, he had dropped to his knees and pleaded with God not to let the nation perish. He felt his prayer had been answered. His sole interest was to sum up what he passionately felt about his beloved country.

With such little time for preparation before the day of dedication, Lincoln worried over his words. He confided to a friend that his talk was not going smoothly. Finally, he forced himself to be satisfied with his "ill-prepared speech." He arrived at Gettysburg the day before the ceremonies in time to attend a large dinner that evening. With Edward Everett across the room, surrounded by numerous admirers, the President must have felt all the more uneasy. He excused himself from the after-dinner activities to return to his room and work a bit more on his remarks.

At midnight a telegram arrived from his wife: "The doctor has just left. We hope dear Taddie is slightly better." Their ten-year-old son Tad had become seriously ill the day before. Since the President and his wife had already lost two of their four children, Mrs. Lincoln had insisted that he not leave. But he had felt he must. With a troubled heart, he extinguished the lights in his room and struggled with sleep.

About nine o'clock the next morning, Lincoln copied his address onto two small pages and tucked them into his coat pocket . . . put on his stovepipe hat, tugged white gloves over his hands, and joined the procession of dignitaries. He could hardly bear the sight as they passed the blood-soaked fields where scraps of men's lives littered the area . . . a dented canteen, a torn picture of a child, a boot, a broken rifle. Mr. Lincoln was seized by grief. Tears ran down into his beard.

Shortly after the chaplain of the Senate gave the invocation, Everett was introduced. At sixty-nine, the grand old gentleman was slightly afraid he might forget his long, memorized speech, but once he got into it, everything flowed. His words rang smoothly across the field like silver bells. He knew his craft. Voice fluctuation. Tone. Dramatic gestures. Eloquent pauses. Lincoln stared in fascination. Finally, one hour and fifty-seven minutes later, the orator took his seat as the crowd roared its enthusiastic approval.

At two o'clock in the afternoon, Lincoln was introduced. As he stood to his feet, he turned nervously to Secretary Seward and muttered, "They won't like it." Slipping on his steel spectacles, he held the two pages in his right hand and grabbed his lapel with his left. He never moved his feet or made any gesture with his hands. His voice, high-pitched, almost squeaky, carried over the crowd like a brass bugle. He was serious and sad at the beginning . . . but a few sentences into the speech, his face and voice came alive. As he spoke, "The world will little note nor long remember . . . ," he almost broke, but then he caught himself and was strong and clear. People listened on tiptoe.

Suddenly, he was finished.

No more than two minutes after he had begun, he stopped. His talk had been so prayerlike it seemed almost inappropriate to applaud. As Lincoln sank into his settee, John Young of the *Philadelphia Press* whispered, "Is that all?" The President answered, "Yes, that's all."

DEPTH, NOT LENGTH

Over 125 years have passed since that historic event. Can anyone recall *one line* from Everett's two-hour Gettysburg address? Depth, remember, not length, is important. Lincoln's two minutes have become among the most memorable two minutes in the history of our nation.

Some of you reading these words may have felt a desire to set aside time to think about what's really important in life . . . to evaluate your use of the hours in your week . . . to pray about specific concerns in your life. Even as you've considered these needs, however, you've convinced yourself that "you just don't have time." After all, what could possibly be accomplished in the ten-, five-, or *two-minute* blocks of time you have to spare?

It might surprise you. With God, the possibilities are limitless.

Recently I heard of a youth leader who mistakenly arrived at a college campus classroom half an hour before he was scheduled to speak. Hating to waste time, he found himself fidgeting. What in the world was he going to do with himself for thirty minutes? *Well,* he thought, *I guess I could pray.* He did. And the vision God gave him for America's youth during that half hour burns undiminished in his soul to this day. His ministry touches tens of thousands of teens every year.

History won't let us forget the day when one man accomplished more in two minutes than another did in two hours. How much more should we not underestimate the power of two minutes with God.

So what if you find yourself with only minutes to spare? Invest them in valuable ends, in enduring goals, in honest conversation with God. Give it your best! Time is like character; it's depth that counts in the long run.

The Best Time to Live Your Dream

One of my long-time friends, Tom Craik, makes his living working as a high school counselor. He's committed to strengthening family relationships, especially helping moms, dads, and kids learn to love each other—which includes accepting, respecting, and communicating with one another.

For years Tom has been in touch with the full spectrum of families in turmoil, so there is not much he hasn't seen or heard. He has never failed to shoot straight with me, a trait I greatly admire. He recently mailed me some musings that I might wish to share with others. Because they are related to our topic, they caught my attention.

"With school having started again, we are probably all aware of what ways we are going to be different this school year. We are going to be different kids this year. We are going to work harder at our studies. This year we'll get A's and B's, be more respectful to our folks, show good sense in all our endeavors so that we will be seen as responsible young adults."

"This year we are going to be more of a family, we are going to be more together, enjoy each other's company more. We are going to like to be with each other. Maybe we'll even go on some weekend outings. As a family we'll argue less and discuss more. We'll respect each other's opinions and talk in a civilized, grown-up, positive, and loving way. We will eat meals together and find out how everyone's day went and really support each other."

"This year Dad will stop drinking and Mom won't yell so much. This year my brothers and sisters will all get along better. We'll help each other with our studies and help Mom around the house. This year Mom and Dad won't have to keep bugging us to do our chores; we'll just do them. We'll keep our rooms clean and put the dishes in the dishwasher. No fights and hassles for us this year. This year we'll appreciate Mom and Dad more because now we really do know all of what they do for us."

"This year I'll be able to go to bed at night and not have to worry about Mom's and Dad's fighting because this year things are going to be different. Because this year I'm going to do better so Mom and Dad won't have any reason to scream and drink and fight. One thing's for sure, we're all going to get along better this year."

Any of this sound even vaguely familiar? Most likely, though, by the time you read this, these "dreams" are going to be history

What is today? A day given to us by the Creator. A twenty-four hour segment of time never lived before and never to be repeated. You may never live to see another day like this one. You may never be closer to a decision you need to make, a step you need to take, a sin you need to forsake, a choice you need to determine. So—do so today. Before the sun sets and tomorrow's demands eclipse today's desires.

as yesterday becomes today . . . becomes tomorrow.

I'm thirty-one years old next month. When I divide that by two, I'm fifteen and a half. Believe it or not, that was just yesterday. Double it and I'm sixty-two. Believe it or not, I think that's tomorrow. Sometime yesterday morning my son was born. Today he's almost a year old. Tomorrow he'll be fifteen. Where does it all go? What's happened to the "dreams"? And you know something else? I know less today than I did yesterday and probably more now than I will know tomorrow. Zoom! There it goes. There I go!

Parents, most of this applies to us. We are the ones who create the atmosphere, the climate in our homes. We create the tension or the peace, the conflict or the order.

We choose whether our homes are loving and supportive or hateful and isolating. We are the ones who teach self-responsibility or blame. We are the ones who look for the good or complain, complain, complain.

Kids, tomorrow you're going to be thirty. The time is already past to look for someone to blame, to look for some reason why things aren't the way you want them to be. Create your own change. Take care of yourself. Act in your own best interest. Work at seeing what you want for yourself and then go about getting it. Find your intention, your purpose, your dream and realize that if it is going to happen, you're the one who's got to make it happen. And then go to it!

Gotta go. My son's looking for the car keys . . .[1]

Tom's right. Painfully right.

Instead of just reading these words, or simply thinking them over, how about our taking the man's advice? The secret lies in how we handle today, not yesterday or tomorrow. *Today* . . . that special block of time holding the key that locks out yesterday's nightmares and unlocks tomorrow's dreams.

Notes

CHAPTER 1
1. Tom J. Fatjo, Jr., and Keith Miller, *With No Fear of Failure* (Waco, Tex.: Word, 1981), 23.

CHAPTER 3
1. William Manchester, *American Caesar: Douglas MacArthur, 1880-1964* (Little, Brown and Company, 1978).
2. Robert E. Coleman, *The Master Plan of Evangelism* (Old Tappan, N.J.: Revell, 1963), 23.

CHAPTER 4
1. Romans 8:29.
2. 2 Peter 1:5-7.

CHAPTER 5
1. Robert M. Pirsig, *Zen and the Art of Motorcycle Maintenance* (New York: Bantam, 1974), 272-273.
2. Ibid.
3. Isaiah 50:7.
4. Proverbs 13:20; 24:30-34; 13:4 and 25:28.
5. Proverbs 27:17.
6. Galatians 6:9.

CHAPTER 6
1. Jenifer Warren, "A Bright Goal Despite Injury," *Los Angeles Times,* 26 September 1985. Used by permission.

CHAPTER 7
1. Matthew 25:40.
2. Anthony Campolo, *Who Switched the Price Tags?*
   (Waco, Tex.: Word, 1986), 69-72. Used by permission.

CHAPTER 8
1. Ephesians 4:24 (RSV).

CHAPTER 9
1. Acts 20:22.
2. Ted Engstrom, *The Pursuit of Excellence* (Grand
   Rapids, Mich.: Zondervan, 1982), 81-82.

CHAPTER 10
1. James 1:13-15.

CHAPTER 12
1. Used by permission of the author.

About the Author

CHARLES R. SWINDOLL, pastor of the First Evangelical Free Church in Fullerton, California, is a teacher to people around the world through his "Insight for Living" radio broadcasts. His other best-selling books include *Come Before Winter and Share My Hope, Living on the Ragged Edge,* and *Strike the Original Match.* Married since 1955, Chuck and Cynthia Swindoll have four adult children.

This booklet was comprised of excerpts from a beautiful devotional book from Multnomah Press titled *The Quest for Character* by Charles Swindoll.

In it you will continue to be launched into a lifelong journey—a relentless pursuit of life's core issues: Courage, purity, honesty, sincerity, and integrity. The deep down stuff that determines who you really are.

Today is more than a square on a calendar. It's an adventure . . . A quest for character that may determine your destiny!

The Quest for Character
by Charles Swindoll

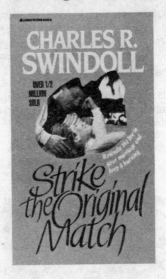

POCKET GUIDES

Action Plan for Great Dads $2.25
Chart Your Way to Success $2.25
Christianity: Hoax or History? $2.95
Demons, Witches, and the Occult $2.95
Family Budgets That Work $2.95
Five Steps to a Perfect Wedding $1.95
Four Secrets of Healthy Families $2.25
Four Steps to an Intimate Marriage $2.95
Getting Out of Debt $2.25
Hi-Fidelity Marriage $1.95
How to Talk to Your Mate $2.95
Increase Your Personality Power $1.95
Landing a Great Job $2.25
Make Your Dream Come True $2.95
Maximize Your Mid-Life $1.95
Preparing for Childbirth $2.95
Raising Teenagers Right $2.25
Sex, Guilt & Forgiveness $2.95
Single Parent's Survival Guide $1.95
Six Attitudes for Winners $2.95
Skeptics Who Demanded a Verdict $2.95
Strange Cults in America $2.95
Surefire Ways to Beat Stress $2.95
Temper Your Child's Tantrums $2.95
Terrific Tips for Parents $2.95
The Best Way to Plan Your Day $2.95
The Perfect Way to Lose Weight $2.25
When the Doctor Says "It's Cancer" $1.95
When Your Friend Needs You $2.25
Working Mom's Survival Guide $2.25
Your Kids and Rock $2.95

Available at your local Christian bookstore or by
mail. Send your check or money order plus $1.25
for postage and handling to:

   Tyndale D.M.S., P.O. Box 80, Wheaton, IL 60189
Prices subject to change. Allow 4-6 weeks for
delivery.